Victorian and Edwardian

RAILWAY TRAVEL

from old photographs

1 Caledonian Railway Conner, 8 ft.
2-2-2 locomotive No. 87

Victorian and Edwardian

Railway Travel

Introduction and commentaries by
JEOFFRY SPENCE

B.T. BATSFORD LTD
LONDON

*For those who never found it necessary to
pretend they were thirty-nine for the next
fifteen years, but have for long been able to
sit back contentedly and remember some of the
things they knew when young.*

First published 1977
Copyright Jeoffry Spence 1977

Filmset by Servis Filmsetting Ltd, Manchester
Printed in Great Britain by
The Anchor Press Ltd, Tiptree, Essex
for the publishers B.T. Batsford Ltd
4 Fitzhardinge Street, London W1H 0AH

ISBN 0 7134 0639 9

Contents

Acknowledgments

I am much indebted to Mr Anthony Lambert, who sought out a number of photographs by visiting about as many places and as far apart as those served by that quaint pre-war institution, the Aberdeen–Penzance service, but with considerably greater speed. From his collection I should also like to record Nos 9, 61, 66, 70, 92.

In addition I am indebted to Messrs Gordon Biddle and R.C. Cogger for help and suggestions; and to the following for permission to reproduce photographs: London Transport 7; Railway & Canal Historical Society 55; Gordon Biddle 65, 67; National Library of Wales 51, 82; R. Carpenter 56; J. Cobban 60; A.B. MacLeod Collection 74; H. Snook 81; Radio Times Hulton Picture Library 84, 115, 134, 139, 143; Oxford Publishing Company 91; George Seaton 92; Tonbridge Historical Society 124. From the Publisher's collection 14, 86, 87, 89, 90, 135, 136, 140, 144. The remainder are from the British Railways Board and the publisher's collection.

Introduction

Early railway travel may have had the advantage of speed over the lumbering road coaches, but things cannot have been very comfortable. One knows of the conditions in which many passengers travelled: open trucks exposed to the weather, to smoke and sparks from the engine, to water from springs which dripped persistently from some tunnels. Signalling was primitive and accidents not infrequent. That passengers by road suffered considerably, especially when travelling "outside", cannot be denied; and the state of the turnpike roads was worse than that of even the poorest of railway permanent ways. If the camera had been in common use in the 1830s and 1840s we might have an impressive idea of the first years of passenger travel; the expressions on some of the travellers' faces could have been revealing.

Before the 1870s, accommodation – whether in covered carriages or not – could never have been more than basic. Even first-class would have been bearable only for comparatively short journeys. There were no dining-cars, no sleeping-cars, no corridor trains; very poor lighting and very little heating; and fares, relatively speaking, were much higher than now.

Lighting was by oil lamps, which sometimes had a tendency to leak, or were too high and smoked or too low and went out. Some of the carriages had one lamp between two low-partitioned compartments, and reading must have been almost impossible except by those prepared passengers who procured a personal travelling lamp – generally in the form of a candle in a metal container which could be fastened on to a window, or the upholstery, or even on to one's person, all very dangerous.

Keeping warm was one of the major difficulties, and this was not, of course, confined to railway travel. The householder, particularly of large houses with lofty rooms, was used to spending a great deal of money on coal (three shillings a ton) so that he and his wife, and as many of their brood as were able to squeeze in, could sit round the fire with burning faces and be chilled to the marrow behind at the same time. Therefore, to be frozen while travelling in the depths of winter was to be expected, and a journey of any distance could be a misery (particularly as feet seem to be the first part of the body affected, the cold spreading until one becomes gradually congealed). There were one or two attempts at heating in the early days, but it was about 1852 when the Great Northern Railway introduced – so they later claimed – flat metal footwarmers, filled with boiling water from a special footwarmer hut (as once stood at Braintree on the Great Eastern), or, in some cases, sodium acetate. These were in use until the early part of the century when steam heating from the engine began to be generally installed. In true British fashion, however, there were outposts of obsolescence, and the South Eastern & Chatham had a long, low heating wagon for footwarmers on the up platform at Dorking even after the First World War ended; and the Appendix to their Working Timetable for May 1922 specifically states that footwarmers must be kept in use from 1 November to 31 March for North Kent line trains between London and Maidstone. Two footwarmers were to be placed in each first-class compartment, and one in each second-class, while passengers travelling third-class were, as usual, made to feel inferior by having to grovel and apply for them.

If one excepts such things as the "bed-carriage" of the London & Birmingham Railway's saloon for Queen Adelaide, then the first sleeping-car was brought out by the North British Railway for the East Coast route to London on 31 July 1873, followed on 1 October by the London & North Western Railway, and by other lines with long-distance night trains shortly afterwards. At first these cars, owing to the social establishment, naturally only conveyed first-class passengers. It was 1928 before the Great Western condescended to recognize that third-class persons required sleep.

The passenger who had not brought some sort of rations with him might, with luck, get ten minutes at certain intermediate stations: Swindon, York and Preston were well-known ones. As many passengers had the same idea about the break it could mean an undignified scramble, especially if one elected to try the soup, which was probably scalding. In the 1870s, the Midland Railway started running Pullman cars on which it was possible to serve food, including pre-cooked food and food kept warm − a practice which would scandalize any Government nowadays and bring forth handfuls of Home Office regulations, for in these days of coddling there is little resistance to germs, and everybody would probably go down with food poisoning. The Great Northern brought out the first proper dining-car in 1879 but, because of the lack of corridor communication, passengers had to travel in it to their destination, paying 2s. 6d. supplementary fee for doing so.

Restaurant cars gradually came into general use in the 1880s. The Great Eastern put into service the York–Harwich car in 1891 (No. 102), and they allowed passengers other than first-class to eat as well. The Great Eastern provided some good food, and the price of a luncheon (soup, fish, joint, pudding, cheese and salad and plenty of it) with use of real linen table napkins, was only 2s. 6d.

Trains being without corridors, early travellers had no lavatory accommodation (unless one could afford a family saloon which was fully fitted even in the 1860s). All one could do, if travelling any long distance, was buy an "India-Rubber Urinal for Male and Female Railway Travellers" made by Sparks & Son, and others, and advertised in *Bradshaw*. Whether an example of this device is hidden away in some museum is not known, but it would have been a godsend. One might visualize the hunted look which must have crept into a passenger's eyes when wearing one of these things in a crowded compartment of mixed company, when he had come to the conclusion that it must serve its purpose. However freely it may have been advertised, it could not possibly have been discussed.

In 1892 the Great Western Railway partially solved the problem by putting on a specially built train for the Paddington–Birkenhead service (No. 29). A corridor was provided, but the doors at the end of each coach were locked, and only the guard had a key. However, the corridor's main use was to enable passengers to reach the lavatory. There was sex discrimination, gentlemen being at one end of the coach and ladies at the other. This in itself could have been a source of embarrassment if one turned the wrong way and did not observe where one was going. Nevertheless, this does seem to have been a good attempt on the part of the Great Western to provide an obvious amenity, and corridor trains soon became commonplace.

Communication with the train crew was also a problem. In July 1864, Thomas Briggs was murdered in a North London Railway train, which caused alarm among passengers, especially those travelling alone. The pages of the *Railway Times* and other contemporary railway papers are full of attempts to solve the matter of communication, some of them highly technical and complicated, some merely fantastic. The Regulation of Railways Act of 1868 enforced communication between passengers and guards on all non-stop trains of twenty miles and over. This resulted in a cord being placed, in most cases, along the *outside* of the train, below the gutter of the carriage roof. This was not much help to a passenger who first had to open the window (which would probably stick), and grope about to find the cord (which would probably break) while all the time he was being attacked from behind with a knife. The internal wire, which gradually applied the brake, was adopted generally from about 1899.

By the turn of the century, travelling was pleasurably interesting and exciting – provided one was travelling first-class and did not have to hump one's own luggage. There was a consistent improvement in the services. On the Great Western, the direct line via Castle Cary was opened in 1906, shortening the journey to Taunton and the west by about twenty miles. The *Cornish Riviera Limited* from Paddington to Penzance was one train on which seats could be reserved, price one shilling. On the night train from Paddington a new improved type of sleeper was brought into use in April 1907; the fee was 7s. 6d. on top of the ordinary first-class fare. The third-class tourist fare from Paddington to Penzance was 40s. (at least a week's wages). Cross-country travel, which had been a minor hell for the family man, improved steadily, and it was much easier to travel between centres like Manchester and Plymouth without either going via London or embarking on several nerve-racking connexions on the way. Anglo-Scottish services were speeded up, at least enough to allow a great-aunt of the present writer with good Victorian powers of endurance, to dance away most of an Edwardian night in London, catch the 5.5 a.m. from King's Cross, and arrive in Inverness at 7.40 the same evening in good time for a Highland Ball – an entertainment which in itself requires considerable stamina. No mean feat this.

The seasoned traveller, or even the sensible one, looked up his train times before going on a journey: in *Bradshaw* if he could find his way round its mysteries, and had enough fingers to leave in pages where he had to change or had an alternative route; or the *ABC* if he knew only his destination and did not want to use his imagination. For *Bradshaw* revealed hidden joys, idiosyncrasies of the different railway companies. "Stops to set down first-class London passengers only" if you were in that status, or by slow train if not; "arrives 3 minutes *earlier* on Tuesdays and the third Saturday of the month"; and, most alarming to the mid-Victorian traveller, "Carriages detached – the Train does not Stop". A slip carriage being detached at speed at Chesterfield is shown in No. 142.

Women's Lib or not, the ladies were not expected and, indeed, not allowed to work out a prospective journey from a timetable. They could not, in fact, cope with the changes of carriage that might be anticipated, or the endless notes, nor know whether the London & North Western was believed to run a better service than the Midland. It is only fair to add that they were given little chance of showing their abilities. But even today, with so many regular-interval services and absence of complexities, there is something rather irritating to us chauvinistic males about the sight of a woman standing haughtily in the circulating area of a big station, telling us firmly what time the train goes, which platform, where to change, and even the time of arrival at the destination; it makes a bad impression on our younger children. The supervising of packing for the family could however always safely be left to the ladies. There was so much to take in the innumerable solid leather suitcases and huge cabin trunks: so many pairs of shoes and so many changes of underwear. How on earth did they pack those voluminous crinoline and bustles? Some of the luggage can be seen in No. 116.

It is sometimes very difficult to pin down a date when doing historical research, and photographs concerning railways are no exception. The serious delay that must have occurred to traffic by the washout of the bridge at Selham, London Brighton & South Coast Railway (No. 133) – reputedly December 1886 – does not appear in London newspapers and one might quite reasonably suppose that this was due to some local weather freak. (There were plenty of other verbose entries in *The Times* index, such as: "Accident to Edward Hewitt, by Alighting from a Railway Carriage before it reached the Platform, Fell over the Parapet into the Road, at Hammersmith.") Research students who go through files of even *The Times* will know, however, that unless someone died in agony, and there was an awful lot of blood and thunder, no one was inclined to take very much notice of ordinary news. The Victorians were extremists in many ways. If it was not a screaming headline about, at best, "Frightful Accident to London Train" (one passenger bruised) or, at worst, "Man Disembowelled by Buffer of Engine" it was the heart-rending scene of a pretty, curly-headed small boy in night-shirt and bare feet (feet were always bare in Victorian drama) reciting "Gentle Jesus" kneeling by the bed of his ageing, haggard mother who was dying of some hideous, unspecified disease. Tears were the order of the day!

In a book of this nature, there is a certain amount of compromise between providing correct and accurate information for the railway enthusiast and satisfying the needs of people who simply like poring over old photographs, noting the strange hats and habits of their forefathers, stirring old memories of Epps's Cocoa or Hudson's Soap and admiring the look of a locomotive or the quaint posters. In the photograph of Homerton station on the North London Railway (No. 79) there is a poster advertising an "improved train service" to Llandrindod Wells, and it seems unlikely that many people would have been encouraged by it to travel between these two points; Homerton was not exactly a well-to-do area in Victorian and Edwardian days. One might question just how much money was (and is) wasted on unnecessary advertising.

It is always dangerous, as we have seen, to state categorically the date of a photograph if there is any doubt. In the same photograph of Homerton, which is an old official one, but undated, a powerful magnifying-glass showed a Charity Match poster to be dated 14 July 1898. This was lucky, for to have guessed would have brought swift retribution from those (many) people who would otherwise have gone to great lengths to have found out when – according to the newsvendor's sheet – Santiago surrendered. One of the faults of the human race is its triumph on finding other people in the wrong.

Trains are an essential part of railway travel, and although some effort has been made to include the more social side, this was not always possible. Except for the occasional driver or fireman, comparatively few people thrust their heads out of train windows. But the choice of photographs was not always easy. No matter how far one casts the net, there is always a dearth of the particular kind of shot one would like. Occasionally a photograph would make an unexpected appearance. The Great Western locomotive *Ganymede* photograph (No. 30) was found on the lavatory wall of a vicarage, where a one-time incumbent had apparently spent many hours of solace, looking at his display of railway prints and photographs, and possibly even working out his sermons. (Did he perhaps have a noisy family?) There is a curious relationship between trains, music and clergymen which has never been satisfactorily explained.

Rolling-stock, too, has been included as being a familiar part of travel, from the comfort of the first-class (No. 46) to the basic austerity of some of the thirds (No. 48). As long ago as the 1890s the London & South Western showed some consideration for its customers by providing well-padded upholstery (No. 49).

Of interest, although available to only a limited few, are the special coaches, like that built for the 3rd Duke of Sutherland (No. 47) who did so much to help open up the far north of Scotland,

and built and opened – without any nonsense about Acts of Parliament or a Royal Assent – his own railway of about fifteen miles, which later formed part of the Inverness–Wick line.

Most railways in Britain had a good record of freedom from serious accidents and they were naturally never keen to advertise failures. For all that, there was, and still is, a small risk of being involved in an accident if one travelled in a train, and a few of these have been shown under the general heading of Misfortunes. The photograph of a snowplough (No. 126) shows one way of removing the cause of troublesome delay; the only other way of removing snow, and often of necessity resorted to, was manpower.

Photographs of staff are included because nobody appears to have produced any major work on railway uniforms, and a good deal of information is slipping away. What pride in dress some of the early railwaymen had. The studies of the Cambrian Railways guard (No. 95) and the Lancashire & Yorkshire's Blackburn station-master (No. 93) – even if his trousers do appear a little too baggy – show them as they appeared on duty. They were well-known and respected members of the community. One of the things that people of an older generation feel, with some regret, is that in their youth the booking-clerks and the porters (at any rate in the country towns) were always the same, and they became, in a sense, old friends with whom one would pass the time of day and ask after the latest baby. Now, like the laundryman, the postman and the milk-man, not only do they appear in their own good time, but there is a constant flow of ever-changing faces.

Things are seemingly not what they used to be, but if nothing ever changed there would be little point in enjoying some healthy nostalgia. But it is only in the mind that long-ago scenes remain the same. What a shock one sometimes gets when faced with reality!

2 An impressive sight that must have remained in the memory of many people. This was a London & North Western train about 1895 picking up water at speed at Bushey troughs – with a good deal of overflow

Trains and Locomotives

3   Leeds Northern Railway locomotive *Aerolite* was built by Kitson, Thompson & Hewitson in 1851. This photograph was after the rebuilding of 1869; it was rebuilt several times after that. Before withdrawal in 1935 she hauled the North Eastern Railway Chief Mechanical Engineer's saloon

4 North British train about 1890 climbing the Cowlairs incline – mostly at a gradient of 1 in 45 – from Glasgow Queen Street. The endless rope, later wire cable, worked by a two-beam stationary engine, hauled the trains up until 1908. The rope was slipped off at Cowlairs without the train having to stop. On the downward journey, the engine was detached and special brake wagons attached; during this time tickets were collected and the engine ran round to the rear of the train which it propelled down the incline. The method at least enabled Glasgow to have a virtually smoke-free station

5 Moorswater station, $\frac{3}{4}$ mile by road from Liskeard (Great Western) was the station belonging to the Looe and Caradon Railways. This photograph was probably taken before 15 May 1901 when a 2-mile connexion was made from the Great Western to Coombe Junction on the Looe branch, severely graded and very circuitous. The locomotive *Kilmar*, an 0-6-0 saddle tank, was supplied in 1869 by Hopkins, Gilkes & Co. of Middlesbrough. Passenger trains started in 1879 and the rolling-stock looks as if it might well be of that date. The line runs through scenery still unspoiled

6 Locomotive No. 5 and rail motor of the Lancashire & Yorkshire Railway which worked in the Ormskirk and Rainford Junction areas. This photograph was taken at Ormskirk about 1906

7 The Oxford & Aylesbury (or Brill, or Wotton) Tramway at an unknown date. It ran from Quainton Road on the Metropolitan & Great Central Joint main line to a terminus some way from Brill, and from 1872 until December 1935 ran a passenger service, although judging by the look of the rear passenger vehicle the vans were probably more comfortable. There were two locomotives built by Aveling & Porter, and this one had a spark arrester

8 An Edwardian London, Tilbury & Southend train. Somebody's private carriage has been loaded on to a truck immediately behind engine, No. 39, a common enough sight in earlier days

9 Highland Railway Royal train on the Invergarry & Fort Augustus Railway in Highland days. The line was opened in 1903 and taken over by the North British 1 May 1907. (Courtesy: Anthony J. Lambert)

10 A Great Eastern Cromer to London express descending Brentwood Bank, drawn by a Claud Hamilton class locomotive No. 1847. This was one of the favourite spots for train photography enthusiasts

11 Great Eastern Railway 2-2-2 locomotive No. 284 (Class W designed by Robert Sinclair and built by W. Fairbairn & Co. in 1862). It hauled the train conveying the Prince and Princess of Wales to Wolferton (for Sandringham) after their wedding in 1863. The engine was specially painted cream for the occasion and, in a restrained way, decorated. The later Victorians tended to overdo the decorating of engines, which could sometimes barely work, so jungled were they with greenery and even quite large shrubs

12 The London, Brighton & South Coast Railway Royal train conveying the Prince of Wales to London on 17 July 1899, approaching South Croydon. The new Quarry line, which the company had built to avoid the tiresome South Eastern Railway's traffic is on the right, nearly ready for the opening to Stoat's Nest on 5 November following. To the left is the Oxted line

13 The Wisbech & Upwell Tramway was built by the Great Eastern in 1883–4 and was at one time of great service in the conveyance of agricultural matter. The locomotives were designed by T.W. Worsdell, Locomotive Superintendent, who later went to the North Eastern Railway. The trains never went at a greater speed than 8 m.p.h. The line was closed to passengers from 2 January 1928, but goods were still carried up to 1966

14 The Corris Railway ran from Machynlleth, where this photograph was taken in 1899, to Aberllefeni, $6\frac{1}{2}$ miles away. Opened in sections in 1883 and 1887, it succumbed to the economic crisis of the early 1930s and passenger traffic ceased from 1 January 1931. Goods trains continued to work until 1948

44555. Machynlleth: Corris Railway Train. FF & Co.

15 In 1906 a train from Glasgow and Edinburgh to Perth and Aberdeen, Caledonian Railway (which had been running for many years), was rebuilt as a corridor train called the *Grampian Corridor Express*. This one was hauled by a 140 class locomotive to the design of J.F. McIntosh. Slip carriages were at one time attached for detaching at Crieff Junction (later Gleneagles) and Coupar Angus

16 Wainwright's E class locomotive No. 165 (built 1907 and almost new) heading the boat train from Charing Cross

17 An interesting group of South Eastern & Chatham workers in the early 1900s. The locomotive No. 636 was a 4-4-0 designed by William Kirtley and built by the London, Chatham & Dover Railway (as No. 177) Class M1 in June 1881 at Longhedge. It was withdrawn in March 1912

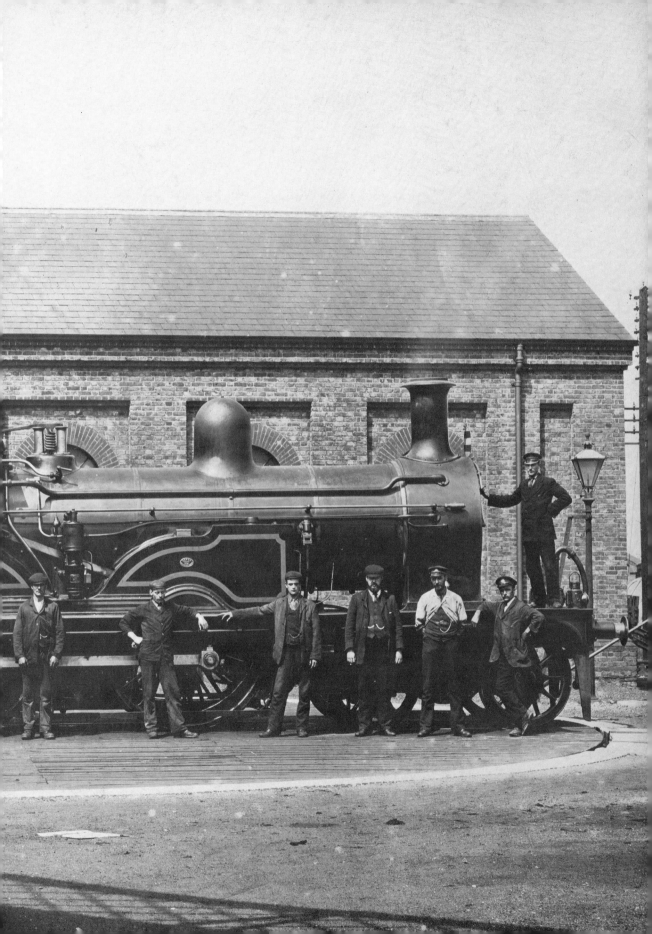

18 London & North Western local train entering Boxmoor & Hemel Hemsted station in Edwardian days. The station has altered its name about half a dozen times since then

19 Caledonian Railway 4-6-0 No. 52 locomotive in Callander station with Oban–Glasgow train. The Freemasons arms on the fallplate above the front buffer beam indicates that the locomotive was driven by a regular driver

20 Excursionists have been catered for since early days. This photograph was taken on the main Brighton line near Balham Intermediate Signal Box of a 23-coach excursion to the south coast. The coaches were mostly four-wheelers and were hauled by B1 class 0-4-2 locomotive No. 180 *Arundel*. The line had recently been quadrupled between Balham and Windmill Bridge Junction, and the running rearranged

21 Caledonian Railway 4-6-0 locomotive No. 49 leaving Glasgow Central
on the 2 p.m. train to Carlisle and
Euston in 1911

22 Webb Compound locomotive with
uncoupled driving wheels for West
Coast Joint Stock about 1892.

23 Midland Railway train in 1896
hauled by a Johnson 4-2-2 No. 181

24 York was entirely a North Eastern Railway centre, but this photograph shows a southbound Lancashire & Yorkshire train leaving

25 London & South Western Railway Beattie 6 ft. 6 in. express passenger locomotive No. 171 built 1859–60

26 Waterloo about 1910. Both the locomotives are Adams 4-4-2T

27 A South Eastern Railway Cudworth 2-4-0 locomotive (No. 130) of the 118 class built 1863. The date of the photograph is uncertain, but the precocious-looking child in fur hat and frilly drawers might provide a clue

28 Above Going to work on the London, Chatham & Dover Railway was not quite Great Western or London & North Western style; there was always a rather poverty-stricken, if spirited, air about the line. This photograph of a train of six-wheelers was the way one travelled if one lived in some parts of Kent. It is drawn by a Kirtley 4-4-0 No. 12, Class M3, built at Longhedge in December 1895, became South Eastern & Chatham No. 471 and was withdrawn October 1926

29 **Below** The first Great Western corridor train, with lavatory accommodation, made its appearance on the 1.30 p.m. Paddington to Birkenhead run on 1 October 1892. The locomotive is of the 3001 class built in 1892 at Swindon and designed for working west of England expresses

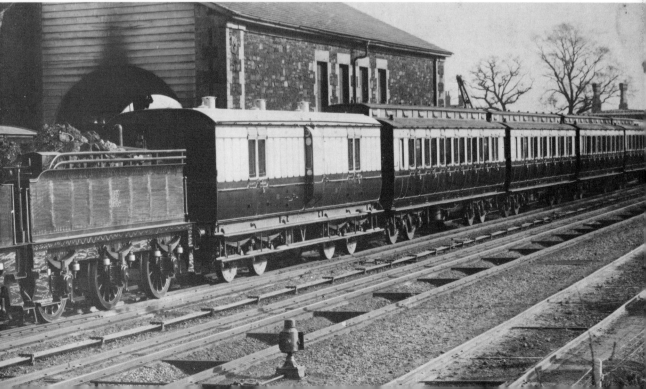

30 Great Western Railway locomotive *Ganymede* of the Firefly class. It was built by Fenton, Murray & Jack of Leeds, delivered July 1841, rebuilt April 1863, and finished its work in August 1878

31 A long way from its own territory, Caledonian Railway locomotive 903 hauling a West Coast train past the Crewe Alexandra Ground on 23 June 1909

32 One way of travelling was in the luxury of a Pullman car. One of the famous all-Pullman trains was the *Southern Belle*, which was put into service 2 November 1908 (first-class only) and ran two services daily between Victoria and Brighton in one hour. It was re-named *Brighton Belle* on electrification in 1933 and finally discarded. This train was headed by No. 326 *Bessborough* produced by D.E. Marsh. The photograph was taken near Balham Intermediate Box

33 Great Western Railway broad gauge train at Flax Bourton, Somerset, about 1891–2. The track is mixed gauge, and the coaches readily convertible to the standard gauge, which took place in May 1892.

34 Caledonian Railway Conner, 8 ft. 2-2-2 locomotive No. 87, built at St Rollox in 1865. It was rebuilt in 1872 and scrapped in 1894

35 Newhaven Continental Boat train from Victoria in 1908. No. 22 was a 4-4-2T Class I3 designed by D.E. Marsh, built in 1908 at Brighton, and superheated when new. It was withdrawn in May 1951. This view was taken just south of the Merstham Tunnel

36 The last broad-gauge train to Penzance on 20 May 1892. This is Swindon Junction, in spite of the Great Northern Railway advertisement board in the background

37 Another old timer well known to Great Western travellers – Iron Duke class 4-2-2 *Hirondelle*, with 8 ft. driving wheels, built at Swindon. It worked from 1848 to 1873. The guard's shelter at the rear of the tender protected him to a certain extent while he kept watch for any trouble along the train behind him

38 Cudworth locomotive and train at Caterham in 1885. One hopes the South-Eastern Railway did not always handle their goods and parcels traffic by turning things upside down on the platform

39 Lampeter, on the Manchester & Milford line, shortly after the opening of the Aberayron branch, rail motor for which is awaiting, like the passengers, the arrival of the fast Carmarthen train from Aberystwyth. The two ordinary carriages were possibly being returned to Aberayron or put into a siding

Rolling-stock

40 Great Western Railway four-wheeled saloon (known as the Paddington Saloon) built at Swindon in 1884. It was renumbered 9009 in 1908

41 In March 1892 the South Eastern Railway provided, without extra charge, Drawing Room Saloon Cars on certain trains. They were bought from the Gilbert Car Manufacturing Company of Troy, U.S.A., and the first car ran on the Hastings line. This photograph is of the one known as the "Folkestone Car" which ran on several Continental trains to Dover, almost all of which did not call at Folkestone

42 Restaurant Car of the Great Eastern Railway's *Norfolk Coast Express* to Cromer, advertised as "Corridor Vestibuled Luncheon Car Train". The photograph was taken in July 1907 when this completely new train set was built at Stratford. The train ran non-stop between Liverpool Street and North Walsham. The flower arrangement, if well-intentioned, could have been a little more imaginative; it is believed the Great Eastern was the first company to start floral decorations on tables

43 London, Brighton & South Coast Railway first-class saloon of 1881–2, designed by William Stroudley. They were reasonably comfortable, furnished with black leather upholstery, bevelled mirrors and gilt mouldings. Externally there was scalloping along the gutter rails; and the company's coat-of-arms was elaborately etched on the frosted glass of the lavatory windows

44 Highland Railway composite first- and third-class carriage built in 1873 at a cost of £466.

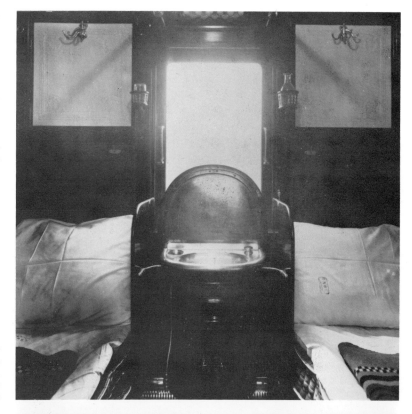

45 Travelling by sleeping-car on the London & North Western's West Coast route started on 1 October 1873. This photograph shows a first-class double sleeper, built at Wolverton about 1900

46 Caledonian Railway first-class compartment of a 65 ft. composite carriage built at St Rollox, Glasgow in 1905. There was a reasonable degree of comfort

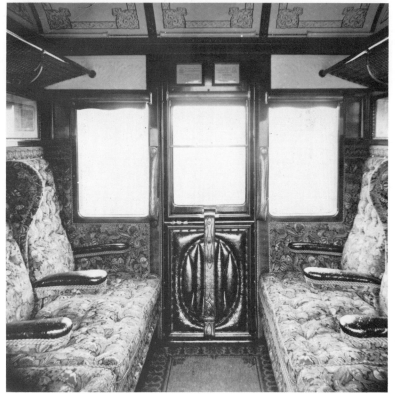

47 A special saloon was built for the Duke of Sutherland in 1899 at Wolverton, to the design of J.C. Park, Carriage & Wagon Superintendent of the London & North Western. It was the prototype for the royal coaches of 1903, and was fitted with Stone's lighting system, with electric bells and ventilating fans. Heat was provided by a hot-water high pressure system stove. There was a main saloon, about 14 ft. long, with figured lincrusta roof in white and gold, and side panelling to match. The rest of the coach consisted of two sleeping compartments, attendant's saloon and minute kitchen. This was the last privately owned passenger vehicle to run on a British railway, as the Duke was the only owner with running powers for his own stock. This, of course, ceased at nationalization

Above main saloon **Below** a sleeping compartment

48 A more austere way of having to travel was by the Lancashire & Yorkshire Railway electric rolling stock built in 1904 for the service between Liverpool and Southport. The company built similar light-weight stock for the Dingle–Southport service which ran partly over the Liverpool Overhead Railway for which the stock shown in the photograph was too heavy

49 London & South Western secondclass lavatory compartment of May 1898. However often one tried to shut it, a lavatory door used to have an unpleasant habit of swinging back and usually ended up triumphantly open

50 London & South Western first-class family saloon of 1898. Victorian and Edwardian families were usually sufficiently large to warrant travelling by this method; it was easier to keep the children in order. There was little rack space, heavier luggage being accommodated elsewhere

Stations

51 The Cambrian Railways station at Montgomery, nearly two miles from the town, which might account for the minor bustle of activity with road vehicles. The architecture does not look the usual Cambrian type, but the neat little train and the double-arm signal (with spectacles half-way down the post) certainly do. (Courtesy: National Library of Wales)

52 Nailsworth, Midland Railway, in 1873. The Midland influence is seen in the glass awning. This grey stone station fits well into the Cotswold valley. It was closed to passengers in 1947

53 Built of Purbeck stone, and with standard London & South Western awning, Swanage celebrates, apparently without any junketing and flag-waving, its opening on 30 May 1885. The first train was headed by a Beattie 2-4-0T locomotive No. 209. The station was later extended in similar style and stone

54 An 1855 photograph of Grimsby, Manchester, Sheffield & Lincolnshire Railway, a company which favoured the saw-tooth-edged roof gable. The tripartite window in the left hand platform screen adds some dignity, which is more than can be said of the two lounging figures named as locomotive department representative and station-master

55 Liverpool Road Station, Manchester, original terminus of the Liverpool & Manchester Railway. This is the original passenger booking office and it is believed that the original ticket window is shown in the bottom of the left hand window, and the old clock frame on the wall to the right. This is possible, but it would be a brave man who would state categorically that this was so. (Courtesy: Railway & Canal Historical Society)

56 Austere Midland Railway red-brick "house" type of station at Harvington on the Evesham–Redditch line. The austerity is softened somewhat by the luxurious profusion of plant life. (Courtesy: R. Carpenter)

57 Blackwater on the South Eastern Railway in 1899; a Tudor-type building with diamond-patterned brickwork, later rebuilt. The outsize nameboard bears the supplementary information "and York Town" – if only to let the South Western know they did not necessarily have all the Camberley and York Town traffic, even if it was over twenty miles further. The "Gentlemen" sign, painted on a sort of reverse curve, is unusual and shows signs of artistry

58 Brighton. H.E. Wallis's new iron and glass roof being erected in 1883 over J.U. Rastrick's original wooden roof of 1841. Of interest are some of William Stroudley's four-wheeled carriages. The lamp, too, is unusual

59 Two contrasting stations which adjoined: Basingstoke, with the London & South Western on the left, before the widening in the 1890s, showing the dip in the platforms as access to a barrow crossing; to the right is the terminus of the Great Western branch from Reading, with Brunel overall roof and elliptical openings

60 Rothes, Great North of Scotland Railway, ten miles south of Elgin. It was the terminus of the not very successful Morayshire Railway branch from Orton for four months in 1858, until extended to Dandaleith. The branch was closed in 1866 and Rothes in 1968. (Courtesy: J. Cobban)

61 Kyle of Lochalsh is the west coast terminus of the fine scenic Highland line 82 miles from Inverness. The fishy connexion is obvious, and it is also the nearest point to the Isle of Skye. (Courtesy: Anthony J. Lambert)

62 This large, ugly red-brick (and later painted) building is Westenhanger, South Eastern Railway, in the 1880s, and quite out of place in rural Kent, but surprisingly substantial for that company, even having matching brick platform walls instead of the more usual wooden fence. At the time of writing the station is still open

63 Callander station on the Caledonian Railway, a large and elaborate building constructed of wood. It was enlarged on the opening of the Killin Junction section of the Callander & Oban Railway in 1870. This photograph is believed to be dated about 1875

64 The South Eastern Railway's city terminus at Cannon Street was opened in 1866, the hotel's handsome frontage having been designed by Edward M. Barry. This picture shows it in the early 1870s before the effect was spoiled when the front steps and balustrade were replaced by shops and the Underground station

65 Coventry, London & North Western Railway in later Edwardian times. It is a typical austere LNWR red-brick building of 1904, but the canopy with a curved top is unusual for that company

66 Overleaf The London & North Western station at Birmingham New Street with its fine curved roof. The present station is no longer identifiable as a Birmingham landmark. (Courtesy: Anthony J. Lambert)

67 Hillington, nearest station for Sandringham on the Midland & Great Northern Joint Railway, with its neat timber-framed platform building and striped valance typical of a number of pre-grouping companies

68 Eardisley, a small Midland Railway junction station near the Welsh border in Herefordshire

69 The neat and tidy station at Belper on the Midland Railway in November 1903. The view up the line shows at least five overbridges. The old station, closed 1878, was a short distance south

70 Llandrindod Wells station, London & North Western Railway, early 1900s. (Courtesy: Anthony J. Lambert)

71 Two interesting views of Clapham Junction: **Left** about 1895, with the South Western station to left and the Brighton station to the right, with locomotive *Eridge* No. 271 leaving down main platform with a Portsmouth train. The tall signals have slotted wooden posts. **Right** (about 1903) shows a similar but more distant view; some modernization has already started. The London General Omnibus is a "garden-seat" type, built 1895, with the high-up driver's seat, a direct survival from the road coaches

72 *Left* (**above**) The London, Chatham & Dover Victoria terminus about the time of amalgamation with the South Eastern (1899) (Courtesy: Radio Times & Hulton Picture Library); and **below** the 1909 building. It would be difficult to find a word that would fully describe the squalor of the earlier building, with the Brighton Company's old station – their new station was opened in 1908 – and the Grosvenor Hotel at the end. In spite of the squalor, the LC&D would take you anywhere between Paris and India, according to their notice. Spiers & Pond remained as caterers until Southern Railway days. The later LC&D station was quite restrained compared with the Edwardian-Baroque of the new Brighton station, but it does rather look the sort of thing one would have built as a model, when a child, with Lot's bricks. The Great Western used the station at various periods and was entitled to advertise itself

73 **below** Headcorn, a typical weatherboard South Eastern station of the 1880s, with platelayers apparently relaxing on their trolley. Milepost 56, on the right wall, was still measured by the old route via Redhill

74 **bottom** The original terminus of the Isle of Wight Railway at Ryde (later St John's Road). The date is 1864–5, before the low weather-boards on locomotives were raised to protect (in part) the engine crew. *Ryde* was one of the three original locomotives built for the IOW Railway. The gentleman in the light-coloured suit was presumably indifferent to the grease and dirt that undoubtedly covered the buffer beam. (Courtesy: A.B. MacLeod collection)

75 An unusual close-up of roof detail: the new roof at Charing Cross, which replaced the one that suddenly collapsed on 5 December 1905. A tie-rod failed and a large portion of the roof and station wall crashed on to the Avenue Theatre, killing several people

76 This photograph of Upper Warlingham on the Croydon & Oxted Joint line was probably taken just before the line opened on 10 March 1884. The nameboard bears the legend "Warlingham", which is one thing it was never called

77 The official opening of the Plymouth, Devonport & South Western's Stoke Climsland station for passengers on 2 March 1908. In the days of the East Cornwall Mineral Company the site had been known as Monks Corner Goods. It was renamed Luckett on 1 November 1909 and closed in 1966

78 Lewes station in the 1880s, with a display of Stroudley locomotives, just before the reconstruction of the station and flattening of some of the sharp curves into and through the station

79 North London Railway stations were usually of solid construction. This photograph of Homerton in 1898 shows the station entrance to have been a dignified (and probably draughty) one. The iron stanchions for the handrail in front are dated 1881

80 A station in the heart of Wales that travellers could use, but with difficulty, in 1860: Llandinam, on the Newtown & Llanidloes Railway. There was one train to Llanidloes in the morning, and one back in the evening. And the accommodation left much to be desired. It always remained rural and was closed in 1962

81 An old picture of the South Eastern's Reigate Town station. Not all that much has changed, except for the platforms, which were extended in 1895. The level crossing gates have presumably been renewed, but they still interfere with road traffic, especially on a summer Saturday. (Courtesy: H. Snook)

82 Less remote than Llandinam, this Manchester & Milford station was a long way – at least fifteen miles – from New Quay. The first name was Cross Inn, and served the nearby village of Llanfihangel, but became New Quay Road in 1874, and eventually Bryn Teify in 1916. Hudson's soap advertisements seemed to penetrate everywhere, and there was even a battered Bovril one here. (Courtesy: National Library of Wales)

83 Brockhurst on the Gosport branch of the London & South Western in the 1860s, judging by the disc signal, although this type persisted later here and there. The station was renamed Fort Brockhurst in 1893, and it was from here that a short branch to Lee-on-the-Solent was opened the following year

84 In the lovely Wye valley lies Tintern. Sadly, no passengers have been able to use the station since 1959, but in Edwardian days plenty of them waited patiently for the "local". (Courtesy: Radio Times & Hulton Picture Library)

85 Marchwiel, a neat little station on the Wrexham and Ellesmere portion of the Cambrian Railways in 1895

86 When the Great Northern opened its Enfield branch on 1 April 1871 the area round Winchmore Hill was much more rural than it is today. This is an Edwardian view, when the evidence of horse traffic was still very noticeable

87 The Lynton & Barnstaple Railway about 1908. **Left** Bratton Fleming station. At the top of the approach path is a signpost conveniently showing that one turns left for Arlington and right for Minehead. **Right** Barnstaple Town station with the Lynton train headed by locomotive *Exe*. The platform shows much evidence of rabbit traffic, and Mr T.E. Cook's hamper seen at Bratton Fleming has at any rate got as far as Barnstaple

88 The second station called Keymer Junction on the Brighton line. It was opened a month later than intended, 1 August 1886 (and replaced the earlier station on the Lewes line which had been closed on 1 November 1883). Following heavy October rains in 1886, about 40 ft. of the up platform collapsed, carrying with it the waiting-room. The fact that Keymer village was nowhere near the first station, and even further away from the second (and passing Burgess Hill station on the way) may have prompted some official to suggest renaming it Wivelsfield from 1 July 1896.

89 Tenterden Town station on the Rother Valley Railway (altered to Kent & East Sussex in 1904). The Town station was opened 15 April 1903, on extension from Rolvenden – which had been the Tenterden station, two miles from the town. The line was closed to passengers in 1954 but is now partly reopened as a preserved line

90 Christow, on the Great Western's Teign Valley line from Exeter to Newton Abbot, about 1910. Passenger traffic ceased from 9 June 1958

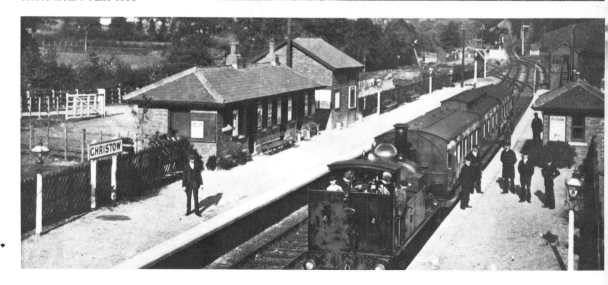

91 Newbury Race Course station in September 1905. This source of traffic was a good money-spinner for the railways

Staff

92 Highland Railway staff: **Left** Stationmaster Macaulay at Helmsdale (Courtesy: George Seaton): and **Right** Guard Donald Campbell (Courtesy: Anthony J. Lambert)

93 Lancashire & Yorkshire Railway uniform. The stationmaster at Blackburn holding in his right hand a railway carriage key, which was the right and proper thing to do when posing for a photograph. But were slack trousers the fashion at this, unfortunately, unknown date?

94 Oakham station on the Midland Railway, 1890, and some of the staff being photographed. There are the inevitable advertisements for soap, for Waterloo Round Cakes, whatever they were, and Tower Tea at 1s. 4d. and 2s. a pound

95 Thomas Lewis, smartly turned-out passenger guard on the Wrexham and Ellesmere line of the Cambrian Railways. The photograph was taken in 1895

96 Some of the men who lessened the danger of accident – permanent way staff, London & North Western Railway, at the turn of the century

97 Great Northern Railway guard of the late nineteenth century

98 Mr M.J. Widdowson, London &
North Western Railway, who was Pay
Clerk between London and Stafford and
branches in the 1860s

99 The down platform at Bishops Stortford, Great Eastern Railway, probably in the 1870s. The stationmaster (right end with top hat) strikes a Napoleonic pose, as most stationmasters did

100 Great Northern Railway: James Stirling's 2-4-0 locomotive No. 285 built by the Avonside Engine Company in December 1867. This was taken at Retford. What the occasion was is not known nor, unfortunately, can it be seen what is on the large sheet of paper being ostentatiously held up to the camera

101 Hotel porters at the Euston Hotel, London & North Western Railway, in 1908

102 This is the crew of the dining-car on the Great Eastern Railway's York–Harwich service, described on the roof-board as "Royal Mail Route, Hook of Holland and Antwerp". The car was introduced in the early 1890s

103 A group of foremen from the Midland Railway's Derby Workshops in Edwardian days

104 Great Northern Railway group photographed at Doncaster Works about 1875. Locomotive 513 (left) was one of Stirling's 0-4-4 Well tanks built at Doncaster in 1874. No. 276 (centre) was built in 1867 and came out in Stirling's first year of office, but appears – by the chimney – to be a Sturrock locomotive. On the right is part of No. 132, a Stirling 0-4-2 Well tank built in 1870

105 The London & South Western staff at Woking about 1875. No explanation is offered for the third figure from the left

106 This photograph was believed to have been Horsham in 1859, but it has been proved to be Guildford, rebuilt to station drawings, in 1883. The bridge in the left background is Farnham Road bridge. The view is looking towards what was No. 2 platform (both faces), now No. 3 of 3/4 island platform; it is, of course, prior to renumbering

107 London & North Western staff at the turn of the century. Left to right: Stationmaster, Guard, Ticket Collector, Train Attendant

London & North Western staff at the
turn of the century. Left to right:
Signalman, Shunter, Loco. Department
driver's overcoat cap and cover, and
Messenger's oil cape

108 Overleaf Stroudley A class loco-motive *Ashtead* at Sutton with various members of staff, March 1886. *Ashtead* was built at Brighton in 1875 and sold in 1937 to the Weston, Clevedon & Portishead Railway, eventually becoming Great Western No. 6. At this date it was fitted with brushes at the front for sweeping snow off the rails

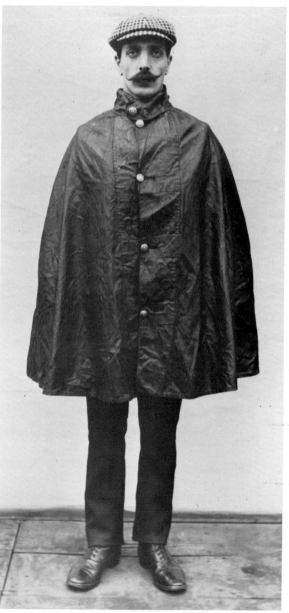

Omnibuses

109 A London & South Western Railway express omnibus between Exeter
and Plymouth of the early 1900s

110 The Great Eastern Railway also ran a number of omnibus services. These two were built at Stratford Works and began operating from Lowestoft to Southwold and to Oulton on 18 July 1904. Outside companies took over the services in 1913

111 Three Saurer charabancs of the North Eastern Railway at Scarborough 1905

112 Scott Sterling Omnibus, North Eastern Railway, at the opening of the Beverley–Driffield service, October 1903

113 The first road motor car run by the Great Western Railway on the Helston–Lizard service on 17 August 1903

114   The Royal Blue Coach service ran
between the Holmesley station of the
London & South Western Railway and
Christchurch and Bournemouth before
the main line was completed between
Brockenhurst and Christchurch on 5
March 1888. It was an old service that
had run from Holmesley (named Christchurch Road until 13 November 1862)
to Christchurch. Bournemouth hardly
existed at the time

115 One way of getting between London termini in 1857: Metropolitan Saloon Bus, which competed with the London General Omnibus Company for two years. There were two rear doors; and as opposed to the LGOC "Knifeboard" bus, the seats on the roof faced each other. (Courtesy: Radio Times Hulton Picture Library)

116   London & North Western Railway "small horse bus" at Euston 16 June 1898. It seems incredible nowadays that passengers would take such weighty pieces of luggage – and bicycles – for, no doubt, a silver threepenny piece as a tip to the porter who manhandled everything up the length of the platform and loaded it all on to the bus. That the ladies could get themselves and their skirts inside such a small space makes one wonder if a quart could, after all, be got into a pint pot

Misfortunes

117 A military train which came to grief on 11 February 1903 at Gomshall & Shere station on the South Eastern & Chatham Railway. The locomotive was Class O, No. 284. In spite of the damage, casualties were light

118 The Great Western seems to have been unlucky with flooding. This was in November 1894, near Kennington, Oxford – a notorious flood area. The platelayers trolley was one way of getting about

119 The picture of flooding on the Great Western at Hereford Barton station in 1886 must have been as bad as it looks if one could take punts out. It would be idle to speculate whether the crowd on the platform were sightseers or people hopefully waiting for a belated train. Barton station was closed to passengers in January 1893 and traffic diverted to Barrs Court

120 The freeze-up in the winter of 1894–5 gave a chilly look to the cutting at the east end of Box Tunnel, Great Western Railway

121 Floods at Stratford on the Great Eastern Railway, December 1903

122 What the sea could do to the Admiralty Pier at Dover. As the photograph is dated late 1870s it was probably the same storm that brought down a considerable area of cliff near Martello Tunnel on 12 January 1877. In the distance is the wooden trestle bridge carrying the main South Eastern line to London. The trestle lasted until 1927 when it was replaced by an embankment behind a concrete sea-wall

123 Result of the South Eastern Railway accident at Staplehurst, 9 June 1865. The up boat train, which in those days ran at varying times according to the tide, had been forgotten by gangers doing work on the Beult River Viaduct, and most of the train was derailed where two rails had not been replaced. Ten passengers were killed. Charles Dickens was a passenger in the carriage standing forlornly on its own, but escaped injury. He never really recovered from the effects and died five years later to the day

124 A collision on the South Eastern Railway at Sevenoaks on 7 June 1884. (Courtesy: Tonbridge Historical Society)

125 The Midland Railway accident at Wellingborough 2 September 1898. A luggage trolley ran off the platform into the path of a Manchester express, which was derailed, killing six

126 Winters are not, it seems, what they used to be. One of the hazards was heavy snow. This is a photograph of Midland Railway locomotive No. 2073 with snowplough attached, taken at Hellifield in November 1904. The Settle and Carlisle line was subject to severe blizzards at times

127 Broad-gauge Great Western engine *Rob Roy*, drawing the up night mail from New Milford, after collision with a cattle train near Awre Junction, Gloucestershire. The main casualties were cattle, but the guard was killed and two drovers "when picked up were mangled and quite dead". The date was 5 November 1868

128 A spectacular boiler explosion on the North Eastern Railway about 1860

129 The Grantham accident on the Great Northern Railway has been described as the "Marie Celeste" of the railway. The East Coast Mail, scheduled to stop at Grantham, failed to do so on the night of 19 September 1906, and was derailed where the Nottingham line diverged. The driver and fireman, experienced men, were both killed, together with eleven passengers and a postal sorter. No one has ever satisfactorily solved the mystery, made even more sinister by the fact that the signalman in the south signal-box had seen them, barely half a minute earlier, standing in their normal positions on either side of the footplate as if everything was as usual

130 The London & North Western were unlucky with the accident at Chelford, Cheshire on 22 December 1894. Fourteen people were killed when, due to high winds, a wagon was blown out of a siding, which set up a series of circumstances culminating in the derailment of an express from Manchester

131 An early motor accident and a foretaste of what was to come with the red harvest of the roads: wreck of a North Eastern Railway omnibus at Thirsk, Yorkshire, on 8 September 1906

132 Grim remains brought up from the mud: one of the girders of the ill-fated Tay Bridge, containing parts of the train which fell with it on 28 December 1879

133 Washout of a bridge at Selham, near Midhurst, London Brighton & South Coast Railway, December 1886

Arrivals
and Departures

134　Special trains to Windsor loading up at Paddington. The occasion was King Edward's garden party

135 The 1911 strike seems to be complete at Paddington, with its crowded platform and deserted tracks. The passengers look so patient that it might be thought they had just been promised an immediate arrival of their train

136 Hop pickers were one of the familiar sights of summer in the south-east up to the Second World War, before machinery more or less replaced them. They enjoyed their paid holidays, even if they had been accommodated in the South Eastern & Chatham's most out of date rolling-stock. Here they are returning to London from a dock at a station in Kent

137 Outside the London, Brighton & South Coast station at London Bridge in late Edwardian days: children of professional theatrical artists line up with their spades and buckets waiting to get on the excursion train for a trip to Bognor. The Elevated Electric advertised was the first section of the LBSC electrification, by the overhead system, between Victoria and London Bridge and was put into operation on 9 December 1909

138 The Channel Tunnel was a speculation of some interest to the South Eastern Railway for most of that company's existence. This photograph, taken in 1900 alongside the main line was one of the several abortive attempts to do something about it. On the left is the entrance to Shakespeare Tunnel

139 **Overleaf** London & South Western Waterloo in Edwardian times: the exodus of Londoners to the seaside from Numbers 3 and 4 platforms, and a surprisingly large number of arrivals at Number 2, where a destination board for the outward journey is for "Norbiton, Kingston and Teddington"

140 A shoe-shine in the station approach at London Bridge, 1887. One might wonder what was in those enormous crates on the wagon, the driver of which appears to be a little exhausted

141 The Great Northern Railway Doncaster Carriage Yard on St Leger Day September 1911. Everything is being got ready for the rush after the races, a matter which required accurate administration. All is spick and span – no newspaper blowing about, or cigarette cartons thrown down

142 To travel in a slip coach was convenient for some people who might otherwise have had to wait for a slow train. One snag was that the restaurant car could not be used; another was that one could not be picked up in the same way on the return journey! This slip was off a down train on the Midland Railway outside Chesterfield station early this century

143 Crowded platform at Uxbridge Road station on the West London Joint line in August 1910: passengers on their way to the White City for the Japan–British Exhibition. (Courtesy: Radio Times Hulton Picture Library)

144 Picking up the mail at speed was a common enough sight in 1900 when this photograph was taken at Thirsk, North Eastern Railway. This particular bag was waiting to be picked up by the *Flying Scotsman*